ZELDA FITZGERALD

The Biography

University Press Biographies
University Press
Copyright © 2017
All Rights Reserved
Cover Image:
Zelda Sayre, 1919

Table of Contents

Introduction

Even as a child, Zelda Fitzgerald was independent and headstrong. The chafing restrictions of a typical upbringing in upper-class, small town Alabama simply did not apply to Zelda, who was described as an unusual child and permitted to roam the streets with little supervision. Zelda refused to blossom into a typical 'Southern belle' on anyone's terms but her own and while still in high school enjoyed the status of a local celebrity for her shocking behavior. Everybody in town knew the name Zelda Sayre. Queen of the Montgomery social scene, Zelda had a different beau ready and willing to show her a good time for every day of the week.

Before meeting F. Scott Fitzgerald, Zelda's life was a constant pursuit of pleasure. With little thought for the future and no responsibilities to speak of, Zelda committed herself fully to the mantra that accompanied her photo in her high school graduation book: "Why should all life be work, when we all can borrow. Let's think only of today, and not worry about tomorrow." But for now Zelda was still in rehearsal for her real life to begin, a life she was sure would be absolutely extraordinary.

Zelda Sayre married F. Scott Fitzgerald on the 3rd of April 1920 and left sleepy Montgomery behind in order to dive headfirst into the shimmering, glamorous life of a New York socialite. With the publication of Scott's first novel, *This Side of Paradise*, Zelda found herself thrust into the limelight as the very epitome of the Flapper lifestyle. Concerned chiefly with fashion, wild parties and flouting social expectations, Zelda and Scott became icons of the Jazz Age, the personification of beauty and success.

What Zelda and Scott shared was a romantic sense of self-importance that assured them that their life of carefree leisure and excess was the only life really worth living. Deeply in love, the Fitzgeralds were like two sides of the same coin, each reflecting the very best and worst of each other. While the world fell in love with the image of the Fitzgeralds they saw on the cover of magazines, behind the scenes the Fitzgerald's marriage could not withstand the tension of their creative arrangement. Zelda was Scott's muse and he mercilessly mined the events of their life for material for his books. Scott claimed Zelda's memories, things she said, experiences she had and even passages from her diary as his possessions and used them to form the basis of his fictional works.

Zelda had a child but the domestic sphere offered no comfort or purpose for her. The Flapper lifestyle was not simply a phase she lived through, it formed the very basis of her character and once the parties grew dull, the Fitzgeralds' drinking became destructive and Zelda's beauty began to fade, the world held little allure for her. Zelda sought reprieve in work and tried to build a career as a ballet dancer. When that didn't work out she turned to writing but was forbidden by Scott from using her own life as material. Convinced that she would never leave her mark on the world as deeply or expressively as Scott had, Zelda retreated into herself and withdrew from the people she knew in happier times.

The later years of Zelda's life were marred by her detachment from reality as, diagnosed with schizophrenia, Zelda spent the last eighteen years of her life living in and out of psychiatric hospitals. As Scott's life unraveled due to alcohol abuse, Zelda looked back on the years they had spent together, young and wild and beautiful, as the best of her life. She may have been right but she was wrong about one thing, Zelda did leave her mark on the world and it was a deep and expressive mark that no one could have left but her.

Chapter 1

Early Years

Zelda Sayre was born on the 24th of July 1900, the sixth and final child to be born to Minnie and Judge Sayre. Minnie Sayre was almost forty years old when Zelda was born and as her other children were all already of school age, Zelda became the family pet. Minnie named Zelda after a gypsy queen character in a novel she had read, nursed her until she was four years old and referred to her as 'Baby' for her entire life.

Minnie Sayre, née Machen, was raised in Kentucky, the daughter of a lawyer turned tobacco plantation owner. An artistic woman raised in the privileged circles of Southern society's elite, Minnie dreamed of a career on the stage but was forbidden from pursuing a creative life by her father. Instead, Minnie married a young lawyer, Anthony Dickinson Sayre and set up home in Montgomery, Alabama where her husband gradually rose to prominence as a Montgomery City Court judge.

As a child Zelda was incredibly independent, smart and courageous. Indulged by her mother, Zelda got into all kinds of trouble as a child, even purposefully stranding herself on the roof of her house to orchestrate a rescue by the fire brigade. There were too many years between Zelda and her siblings for there to be easy friendships between them and Zelda seemed to spend much of her childhood largely unsupervised. At school, Zelda was clearly capable but her interest in the monotony of the school day was limited. By the time Zelda had reached adolescence she had found far more engaging things than studying with which to fill her time and used to freedom to go swimming, take herself for ice cream sundaes and explore the outer limits of her town.

Zelda quickly matured into a beautiful young woman. With very pale skin, large eyes and naturally blonde hair, she began using make up at a young age to intensify her already dramatic looks. Zelda practiced ballet and loved to perform at school and community recitals wearing elaborate dresses that Minnie made for her. From the age of fifteen, Zelda attended every dance she could in Montgomery and quickly became the most popular girl in town.

Quoted in a newspaper society article as saying she only cared about two things; swimming and boys, Zelda scandalized her neighbors by wearing a skin-colored one piece swimsuit and dancing cheek to cheek with boys at chaperoned dances. Away from the prying eyes of the community's moral police, Zelda displayed a lack of inhibition and a lust for life that the boys loved and the girls envied. As one of Zelda's many beau's from this time remarked, 'She lived on the cream at the top of the bottle.'

Minnie was known for her vivaciousness and sense of fun, was an avid reader and poet whose work was published in the local newspaper, and had a laissez-faire attitude towards disciplining her children. By contrast, her husband Judge Sayre as he was known by all, was a serious man who had an acute sense of social obligation and propriety. The marked difference between Zelda's parents approach to life and parenting put her in an unusual position. Zelda's mother's lenient parenting encouraged Zelda's wild behavior while her father's impeccable social standing allowed her a certain measure of freedom.

As a member of the ruling class, the 'thoroughbreds' of the genteel south, Zelda was seen as somewhat above reproach and yet the restrictions she faced as a burgeoning 'southern belle' chafed against her naturally flamboyant personality. The tension between the conservatism of the world she was raised in and her innate desire to be wild and free would take its toll on Zelda's mental health in her later years. Minnie's relaxed attitude towards her daughter's reputation was also later criticized by F. Scott Fitzgerald who accused her of doing a 'rotten job' of protecting Zelda against the more predatory males she came into contact with. It is thought that Zelda was pressured into losing her virginity when she was around fifteen years old when she was taken into an abandoned schoolyard by a group of school friends and, possibly, raped.

By the time Zelda reached her senior year of high school in September 1917 her home town was transformed. The First World War was underway and due to America's involvement Montgomery was overrun with young army recruits, training at nearby barracks. Now Zelda had no time for anything but soldiers and she attended parties and dances almost every night of the week. Judge Sayre was concerned for his daughter's reputation but Minnie celebrated her daughter's popularity, vicariously taking pleasure in the small box of military insignia she collected as trinkets of brief infatuations. When Zelda left high school she was voted the 'Prettiest and Most Attractive Girl in Class'.

Chapter 2

Meeting F. Scott Fitzgerald

Zelda first met F. Scott Fitzgerald in July 1918 when he was a first lieutenant in the 67th infantry, training at Camp Sheridan. Zelda was dancing, as she did most nights, at the country club and Scott was immediately enchanted by her looks , her energy and her attitude. Scott himself was a strikingly handsome man who made sure he stood out by going against uniform requirements and wearing bright yellow boots and spurs with his Brooks Brothers tailored uniform. Zelda and Scott looked like a match made in heaven and when they first began dating people even commented that they looked alike.

 Scott was older that Zelda, twenty-three to her sixteen and at the time they met he was merely an aspiring writer with no impressive family background to speak of and no source of income. Born and raised in St Paul's, Minneapolis, Scott was an Irish Roman Catholic and, that summer, he fell deeply and irrevocably in love with Zelda Sayre. Zelda was not short of committed admirers with whom she could spend a wild evening and indulge in a fleeting romance, and if Scott wanted to spend time with Zelda he would have to be ready to compete.

Zelda's feelings towards Scott during the first months of their courtship are difficult to decipher. She encouraged other men to compete with Scott and refused to commit, despite the fact that Scott was expecting to be posted overseas any day to fight for America in the Great War. As the date for Scott's departure loomed the pair wandered in the open air of the pine groves on the outskirts of Montgomery and talked about love, life and art. But Zelda's heart was not yet won and she continued to indulge herself with casual romances that had a dual effect on Scott, infuriating him with jealously but also intensifying his desire for Zelda. For Scott, a big part of Zelda's allure was the desire she provoked from others.

Scott left Montgomery in November 1918, bound for France but just as he was readying to set sail the Armistice ending the war was signed. When Scott returned to Montgomery Zelda was not pleased to see him and he himself felt disappointed by the anti-climax of never actually going to war. Zelda and Scott had basked in the glamorous tragedy of their summer romance, paused, potentially forever, by Scott's call to arms. Scott's return to Montgomery stripped he and Zelda's love affair of its dramatic allure and replaced it with pressure to commit.

Zelda continued her life as the preeminent belle of the Montgomery social scene and, once discharged from the army, Scott moved to New York to pursue his writing career. Zelda agreed that once Scott was established in New York she would join him and they would begin their dazzling, unconventional life together. Zelda and Scott exchanged passionate, poetic love letters in an attempt to keep their affair alive despite the distance between them but while Scott worked a low paying job with an ad agency and papered his walls with rejection notes, Zelda pined for him and distracted herself by dating other men. One such letter from eighteen year-old Zelda to Scott dating from this time reads, "Don't you feel like I was made for you? I feel like you had me ordered – and I was delivered to you – to be worn – I want you to wear me – like a watch-charm or a button hole bouquet – to the world."

Eventually Scott sent Zelda an engagement ring which she wore to her dances, causing a stir in

Montgomery. The letters continued. In many of the letters Zelda teased Scott, asking him not to write so much then chiding him for not being in touch. She hinted that she was still seeing other men and, finally, accidentally sent a letter to a young golfer whose pin she had accepted (a token of affection at the time) to Scott. Scott was furious and confronted Zelda in Montgomery immediately, demanding that she marry him right away. Scott knew that he was '...in love with a whirlwind' and 'must spin a net big enough to catch it'.

Zelda refused Scott's proposal, knowing that it was offered from a place of jealousy and frustration at his lack of success. Shrewdly, Zelda knew that Scott's faith in himself was too unsure for her rely on him and that her bright dream of living an extraordinary life rested solely on the reality of who she agreed to marry. Scott returned to New York feeling crushed and vowed never to bother Zelda again until he was a success. Zelda regretted her decision immediately. Despite her capricious nature Zelda was in love with Scott and she begged him to return to her. And return to her he did, five months later when he had secured a contract to publish his first novel, *This Side of Paradise*, and money in the bank.

Zelda Sayre and F. Scott Fitzgerald were married on the 3rd of April 1920 at St Patrick's Cathedral in New York City. The young couple's wedding party was made up of just eight people with neither set of parents present and their honeymoon was conducted in a suite at the Biltmore Hotel where they drank champagne, ordered room service and enjoyed their first night as a married couple.

Chapter 3

The Newlyweds

Zelda's first days in New York were exciting and disorientating. For a girl who had never seen anything of the world apart from her own small town in the American south, New York was an endless party with no rules or restrictions to hold them back. Zelda described herself and Scott in New York as, 'small children in a great, bright unexplored barn', with no adults around to chaperone them. Both husband and wife loved to shock people with their spontaneous, erratic behavior and it was at this time that Scott undressed at a performance of George White's *Scandals* and Zelda dived into the fountain at Union Square. With *This Side of Paradise* still receiving rave reviews and attention from New York's literary elite, Scott and Zelda were caught up in a whirlwind of publicity. Everyone wanted a piece of the young couple whom Dorothy Parker described as looking as though they had 'just stepped out of the sun.'

With so many demands on his time, Scott struggled to write in New York and Zelda quickly became exhausted, struggling to keep up with all of the drinking and partying that was expected of her. The couple decided to buy a car, a wrecked old Marmon that they drove to their new home in Westport, Connecticut. Zelda was looking forward to being able to swim every day and intended to have people over only on the weekends. Soon though, Zelda and Scott's life in their rented home in Westport began to resemble their life in hotel rooms in New York as a string of friends came down for extravagant parties that lasted for days on end.

In the Fitzgerald home in Westport, publisher George Jean Nathan stumbled upon Zelda's diaries and expressed an interest in publishing them. Zelda was interested but Scott vetoed the suggestion, stating that he used her diaries for inspiration in his own work. Already, Zelda's creative output was being appropriated by her husband. To their close friends, most of whom were in reality Scott's friends, Zelda seemed the stronger of the pair but beneath Zelda's tough and wild exterior she was deeply vulnerable. Zelda seemed to lose control of her own life as her movements were increasingly defined by Scott's schedule. Scott hoped that he would curb his excessive drinking in Westport in order to better focus on his writing but for Zelda, the slow pace of life outside of New York encouraged her to drink more. The pair has furious rows, fueled by alcohol and ill-wishing acquaintances, and the same issue came up time and time again - what was Zelda supposed to do while Scott was writing?

The pace of the Fitzgerald's lifestyle did not abate and Scott and Zelda saw out the year of 1920 in a whirl of dinners, dances, theatre dates and all-night parties. Surprisingly, Scott managed to write a number of short stories and the majority of the novel, *The Beautiful and the Damned,* during this time. A novel that centers on the breakdown of a disastrous marriage, Scott insisted that *The Beautiful and the Damned* was not an autobiographical novel but many of the ideas and some of the dialogue of his female lead character was taken directly from Zelda's spoken and written words. Scott even coined a term for the heroines of his stories, modeled on the original 'mental baby vamp', i.e. Zelda.

After spending a lonely Christmas in New York, Zelda discovered that she was pregnant in February 1921 and returned to Montgomery to visit her parents. While back home in the town she grew up in, Zelda agreed to take part in the annual Les Mysterieuses Ball where she danced with characteristic abandon and sensuality, even showing her underwear to the scandalized crowds.

Intending to find a suitably romantic and exotic place in which to bring their baby into the world, the Fitzgeralds left America for Europe on the 3rd of May 1921. First the couple went to London where they dined with St John Irvine and Lennox Robinson. Zelda donned men's clothes to enjoy a risqué walking tour around London's docklands on a tour of Jack the Ripper's favorite spots. After a disappointing few days in France Zelda and Scott travelled to Italy, hitting Venice, Florence and Rome before returning to the USA. Fitzgerald's opinion of Europe was that it was of 'merely antiquarian interest', boldly stating of New Yorkers, 'we will be the Romans in the next generation as the English are now'.

Zelda and Scott decided that the best place for Zelda to have her baby would be St Paul, Minnesota, Scott's home town. The couple had briefly settled in Montgomery but Zelda found it too hot for her blossoming pregnancy and caused her customary scandal by turning up to the local swimming pool in a tank top when six months pregnant. At the time and in Montgomery, Alabama, women in a 'delicate condition' were generally expected to stay indoors. In St Paul Zelda made one friend, a Mrs Xandra Kalman who gave Zelda some hope of having the life she desired after having children. Xandra also purchased everything Zelda needed to care for her baby, something she had no knowledge of at all.

Chapter 4

A Flapper, a Writer and a Mother

Zelda gave birth on the 26th of October 1921. The labour was long and difficult and although Scott was incredibly nervous for his wife's health, he was a detached presence. Zelda's words on seeing her baby girl for the first time, 'I hope it's beautiful and a fool - a beautiful little fool' were appropriated by Scott and used word for word by his character Daisy Buchanan in *The Great Gatsby*. The Fitzgerald's baby was named Frances Scott Fitzgerald, 'Scottie' for short and although Zelda professed to being completely devoted to her she also admitted to being disappointed about her sex.

Zelda was unhappy in Montgomery with its harsh winter and lacking social scene and she struggled to lose her baby weight in the months following Scottie's birth. The Fitzgeralds could not stay home for long, though and soon lost themselves in weekly hops at the local club and raucous house parties at their home in the centre of St Paul. Around late January/early February Zelda discovered the reason she had struggled so much to lose her baby weight, she was already pregnant with her second child. Mortified at the thought of having another baby so soon after Scottie, Zelda decided to have an abortion. Little is known about Zelda's abortion or the role Scott played in her decision to have one but by late February Zelda was no longer pregnant.

By March the couple had an excuse to return to New York with the publication of Scott's *The Beautiful and the Damned.* The publication of Scott's second novel also gave Zelda a chance to get her own writing in print. Zelda had expressed a desire to pursue painting or dancing or a career in the burgeoning movie industry but hadn't made any attempt to get started. Instead, Zelda began to write. And not just diaries and letters, as she had done her entire life, but articles and stories. Zelda accepted an invitation to review Scott's *The Beautiful and the Damned* and did so in a tone that was decidedly tongue in cheek, noting that she recognized great swathes of prose from her own diary and that people should purchase the book in order that she might buy a new dress she had her eye on.

Zelda also wrote an article entitled *Eulogy of the Flapper* for Metropolitan Magazine in which she laid out the basic rules of flapperdom and her own philosophy for life. Zelda celebrated the young women who 'awoke from her lethargy of sub-dem-ism, bobbed her hair, put on her choicest pair of earrings and a great deal of audacity and rouge and went into battle.' She also made a clear distinction between the imitation flappers parading around small towns all over America and real flappers who embodied the courageous, transient and drama of the original. Zelda also sold two short stories between 1922 and 1923 but they failed to launch her career as a writer in her own right, primarily because one of them, *Our Own Movie Queen*, was published under Scott's name.

The Fitzgeralds moved to Long Island, again trying to separate themselves from the more damaging aspects of their lifestyle in New York. The couple settled in Great Neck, nicknamed the Gold Coast. The Gold Coast had its own elite social scene and the Fitzgeralds soon fell into old ways, driving in and out of New York every weekend and attending wild parties at their neighbors' homes. It was around this time that the Fitzgeralds began spending time with Ring

Lardner, the famous sports writer, and made an appearance in Hearst's International with a full page spread. In Great Neck, the Fitzgeralds were the golden couple, just as they had been during their early days in New York. No one could resist the allure of their sunny charm, their frivolity and their sense of adventure. The Fitzgeralds may have appeared to most casual acquaintances as the heart and soul of the party, angelic visions dusted with gold, but closer friends began to notice cracks in the veneer of their marriage.

At Great Neck Zelda and Scott's marriage entered darker, more difficult territory when Scott's drinking became more extreme. Scott became depressed as he battled with writer's block and reacted by going on two and three day drinking binges in New York of which he had no memory afterwards. Zelda worried about money and put pressure on Scott to earn more in order to fund their lavish lifestyle. In an interview with the Baltimore Sun, Zelda responded to the interviewer's question of what she wanted Scottie to be when she grew up; 'Not great and serious and melancholy and inhospitable, but rich and happy and artistic. I don't mean that money means happiness, necessarily. But having things, just things, objects, makes a woman happy.'

Chapter 5

To The Riviera

In May 1924, Scott, desperate to make some headway with his latest novel, moved the Fitzgeralds to Paris. The Fitzgeralds spent several days exploring the city with a hired nanny looking after Scottie and made the acquaintance of the Murphys, a beautiful and wealthy American couple who acted as patrons to burgeoning artists working in Paris, such as Picasso, Miro and Ernest Hemingway. On the Murphys' advice the Fitzgeralds left Paris and relocated to the South of France at the end of the month. It was off-season on the French Riviera and the Fitzgeralds had no problem finding a villa for rent close to that of the Murphys. Zelda fell in love with the climate in Antibes which resembled that of her childhood in Alabama in the summer and enjoyed the closeness of the sea, the Mediterranean food and their beautiful villa.

Scott finally found the inspiration to make headway with his new novel, a novel that eventually became *The Great Gatsby* as Zelda filled her days with swimming and sunbathing. Soon, though, Zelda became restless. Used to being active and surrounded by friends, Zelda soon tired of lying on the beach and began spending time with a group of young French aviators stationed at nearby Frejus. One pilot in particular, Edouard Jozan, drew Zelda's attention and she began spending almost every afternoon swimming and every evening dancing with him at the local casino. Initially, Scott encouraged the friendship as he and Zelda socialized with the aviators together, having picnics on the beach and excursions along the coastline. But soon it became clear that there was more than friendship blossoming between Zelda and Edouard.

Over the course of six weeks Zelda and Edouard became deeply infatuated with each other. On the surface Scott and Edouard seemed like similar creatures, both young, energetic and handsome, but underneath they were each cut from completely different cloth. Where Scott was intellectual, metropolitan and obsessed with money, Edouard's background was provincial and his approach to life was a romantic quest for glory. Deeply tanned, tall and muscular, Edouard was a natural leader and resembled the boys who had fought for Zelda's affection when she was still a young debutante in Montgomery.

Many men had fallen in love with Zelda but now, for the first time, Zelda was seriously reciprocating the attention and went as far as to ask Scott for a divorce. We know little about the ensuing 'Big Crisis'. It's unclear whether Zelda was sexually unfaithful to Scott or not but it is clear from the snippets of information we can glean from Scott's ledger and letters that something serious had occurred. Serious enough to damage the Fitzgeralds' marriage in some unrepairable way. Yet to the outside world all appeared normal. A visit from friends, the Seldeses, in August this year, just weeks after the 'Big Crisis,' seemed to pass without a hitch. The Fitzgeralds were presenting a united front.

This united front completely gave way at the beginning of September when Zelda attempted to commit suicide. Scott arrived, ashen-faced, at the Murphys' door in the middle of the night and begged for their help to save Zelda who had swallowed a bottle of sleeping pills. The Murphys stayed up with Zelda, convincing her to walk up and down all night and quite possibly saving her life. In the weeks following Zelda's suicide attempt Scott focused single-mindedly on completing his latest novel. Unsure what the call the novel and considering *Trimalchio* and the *High-Bouncing Lover*, Zelda came up with the name, *The Great Gatsby*. At the end of October the manuscript was complete. Scott sent *The Great Gatsby* to Scribners and he and Zelda left the Riviera, where the weather had grown cold, and headed to Rome.

In Italy Zelda became ill with colitis, a painful condition that creates inflammation and infection in the colon and may have resulted in some part from the emotional turmoil of her failed love affair. While recuperating, Zelda took up painting. The Fitzgeralds moved on to Capri but their time in Italy was destructive and unhappy and soon they returned to Paris. In April 1925, the Fitzgeralds first began spending time with Ernest Hemingway. Hemingway and Scott bonded over their writing, their drinking and their experience of being literary Americans in Paris. Physically strong, talented and having been injured seriously injured on the Italian Front during the First World War, Hemingway represented a masculinity that Scott admired.

This masculinity, by contrast, repelled Zelda who disliked Hemingway from the outset. Zelda described Hemingway as 'bogus', as presenting the world with a certain macho air that was artificial and forced. For once, Zelda was not the person Scott turned to for advice on his work and she was angered by Hemingway's coarse ways and opinion that women should serve their husband's intellectual endeavors and pursuit of pleasure over their own. Zelda accused Hemingway of being homosexual and of criticizing her while borrowing money from Scott. Her suggestion that Scott and Hemingway were indulging in a homosexual affair marked the second most serious rift in the Fitzgeralds' marriage.

Zelda's dislike of Hemingway was thoroughly reciprocated. On his first meeting with Zelda, Hemingway is thought to have told Scott that she was crazy. Later Hemingway included the Fitzgeralds in his autobiographical work, *A Moveable Feast*, and pulled no punches, taking time to explain how Zelda sabotaged Scott's writing by encouraging him to drink and take her to parties. He wrote, 'Zelda did not encourage the people who were chasing her and she had nothing to do with them, she said. But it amused her and it made Scott jealous and he had to go with her to the places. It destroyed his work, and she was more jealous of his work than anything.'

Chapter 6

Hollywood, California and Wilmington, Delaware

Despite being surrounded by the 'Lost Generation' of expatriate writers who included Gertrude Stein, Robert McAlmon and Alice B. Toklas, Fitzgerald could not write in Paris and so left with Zelda and Scottie in March 1926 for the Riviera. A few months later the Hemingways joined the Fitzgeralds, the Murphys and the MacLeishes and settled in for the Summer.

Even now, Zelda found her lust for life in defying expectations and inviting danger and scandal into her life. One night she danced at the casino in an impromptu and arresting performance, during which she held her skirts up above her waist. On another occasion she dared Scott to dive off the top of a thirty-foot cliff into the sea below with her, despite the mass of dangerous rocks just under the surface. The Fitzgeralds were still at their peak. Zelda was beautiful and not yet subsumed by the breakdowns that would later destroy her and Scott was one of the most popular and successful fiction writers of the day.

That summer Zelda's health took a turn for the worse and she had to have her appendix removed. Her colitis flared up again and she experienced undefined ovarian issues. Over the whole of 1926 Zelda's health was troublesome and by the end of the year the couple decided it was time to move back to the United States. Zelda had little to show for the two years the Fitzgeralds had spent in Europe. She had not written, nor had she painted and her love affair with Edouard was nothing but a painful memory.

On a handful of frightening occasions, Zelda had also lost complete control of her emotions. One such incident occurred in a restaurant when, supposedly jealous over the attention Scott was giving to dancer Isadora Duncan, Zelda threw herself down a flight of stairs. The Fitzgeralds were almost penniless, Scott had not succeeded in writing another novel, although he was partway through the novel that would become *Tender is the Night*, and yet he insisted that Europe had been a great success.

On their return to America, Scott took a position with the United Artists in Hollywood. Scott was tasked with writing a screenplay for the famous actress Constance Talmadge and at first Zelda was enthusiastic about the move. If Scott's script was a success they would make a large sum of money and Zelda hoped that her life at the Ambassador Hotel would involve glamorous parties and rubbing shoulders with the greatest stars of the day. In reality, the stars in Hollywood kept largely to themselves and worked on their vocation, something Zelda sorely lacked.

That Zelda was idle had become a source of discord in the Fitzgeralds' marriage. While working for United Artists, Scott had met the seventeen year old star Lois Moran. Lois was young and innocent and almost always chaperoned by her mother but Zelda was jealous of the high esteem Scott held for the star. During a heated argument Scott defended Lois against Zelda's attacks by praising her for having a career that she worked hard at. Something, Scott reminded Zelda, she had never done.

After eight weeks of hard work, Scott submitted his script only to have United Artists reject it. It was time for the Fitzgeralds to find themselves another home but this time Zelda wanted a place they could call their own. The couple settled on Wilmington, Delaware, a quiet, archaic town close to the Delaware River. Here the Fitzgeralds rented Ellerslie, an enormous but elegant mansion with sweeping gardens and a pillared portico. The move to a palatial home of their own was supposed to bring tranquility to the Fitzgeralds' life and aid Scott's writing which had come to a complete standstill. Yet, even on the train ride east, Zelda and Scott had a furious row, perhaps caused by Scott's invitation to Lois Moran to visit them in Delaware, and Zelda threw her diamond and platinum wrist watch out of the window.

Zelda embraced the fresh start Wilmington offered and began to write again. In 1927 Zelda wrote four articles, three of which were published in 1928. In one article, *Looking Back Eight Years,* Zelda looked back at the Fitzgerald's lives before widening her lens to include the entire post-war generation. The disappointment of this generation, she wrote, came not from meaningless prosperity or even instability but from longing for an adult life that had the same poetic intensity of their youth.

The Fitzgeralds could not last long without the delirious distraction of a wild party and soon they were back to their old ways. Friends motored in to Wilmington for long weekends, during which the Fitzgeralds sometimes spun completely out of control, evidenced by letters of apology Zelda would distribute after a particularly bad drunken performance. For the second time Zelda lost control of her emotions completely and could only be calmed by a shot of morphine from a local doctor.

By the time summer came back around again Zelda had found her vocation and dedicated herself completely to dance. Zelda became a student of Miss Littlefield in Philadelphia when she was aged twenty-seven, an advanced age to begin studying to become a ballerina. In order to practice at home Zelda installed a huge mirror on the floor of one of their drawing rooms with a ballet bar in front and practiced her dance moves hour after hour.

Tension in the Fitzgerald's marriage was exasperated that Autumn by a visit from Hemingway and his new partner, Patricia Pfieffer. Hemingway and Patricia had a baby boy in tow whose presence was painful for Zelda. Zelda had suffered from repeated pelvic infections and was unable to conceive the baby boy the Fitzgeralds desperately wanted. Suffering from the strain of their damaged marriage, which by this time had lost all physical elements, Scott turned ever more obsessively towards alcohol.

Scott failed to write anything of note for the entirety of 1927. The novel he had been working on since 1925 was still far from finished and would not be published until 1934. Fed up with life in Wilmington and perhaps embarrassed by a terrible scene they had caused during a visit from Zelda's sister Rosalind Smith, during which Scott slapped Zelda so hard he made her nose bleed, the Fitzgeralds moved back to France. They had been happy in Paris and so tried to retrace their steps and find a place where they could be at peace.

In Paris Zelda practiced her ballet for eight hours a day, determined to become a professional ballerina. The summer moved slowly with both Scott and Zelda feeling listless, distant and, yet again, drinking too much. By September 1928 the Fitzgeralds were back in Wilmington and living in their Ellerslie mansion where Zelda continued with her ballet in front of the mirror for 8 to 10 hours a day. Scottie, although cared for by a nanny seemed to be neglected emotionally by both parents during this time as both pursued their individual passions and brooded and circled the dissatisfaction they felt in each other. Once the lease on Ellerslie was up the Fitzgeralds resorted to their usual fix for problems and ran away from them. In the Spring of 1928, the Fitzgeralds with their few personal possessions packed in trunks, boarded a ship for Genoa.

Chapter 7

Ballet and Breaking Down

The Fitzgeralds settled back in Paris where Zelda immediately restarted her lessons with Lubov Egorova, head of the Diaghlev troupe ballet school and former star of the Ballet Russe. Despite Zelda's dedication to her art, Scott would not share her illusion that she would ever become a first-rate ballet dancer. Having started so late there were limits to what Zelda might achieve and yet she dedicated herself to her goal so single-mindedly that she could not fail to improve. Scott saw in Zelda's dancing a protest to their life together and a defiance against his stab at her idleness during his infatuation with Lois Moran. In retaliation he turned ever more destructively to alcohol.

Scott was able to fund the Fitzgeralds' extravagant lifestyle by writing short stories but he began to hate himself for his inability to complete a novel that could match *The Great Gatsby.* While Scott descended into inactivity, shamed by his close friend Hemingway's more prolific output, Zelda entered the most productive period of her life. As well as her grueling ballet schedule, Zelda began writing again and started work on a series of six short stories that looked at the lives of six different women. College Humor agreed to publish the stories but Scott insisted that he edit them and that they be published under both of their names.

For the final story of the six entitled *A Millionaire's Girl,* Scott tried to negotiate a higher price. Scott insisted that this story was the best of Zelda's and on that basis should be worth more. For Zelda's other stories College Humor had paid $250 or $500 dollars. The magazine agreed to pay $4000 for *A Millionaire's Girl* if Scott's name alone appeared on it and he agreed. The stories attracted critical attention and were considered rich and evocative despite, or perhaps because of, the fact that they were written while Zelda hovered on the precipice of a complete mental breakdown.

The difference between the Fitzgeralds' public persona, that of the glamorous party-going flapper and the philosopher novelist, and the reality of their day to day existence at this time was startling. Zelda was invited to dance professionally for the first time in Nice. Although a minor success for a professional dancer, this opportunity spurred Zelda on to dedicate even more time and energy to her classes and as the intensity of her ballet obsession increased her mental health declined.

In Paris both of the Fitzgeralds were isolated from each other and society at large, unable to communicate properly in Parisian circles but equally ill at ease amongst the showy expatriate Americans that descended upon Paris in droves in 1929. It was with great excitement that the Fitzgeralds escaped Paris again to spend the summer in the Antibes, close to their friends, the Murphys even though Zelda was remote and Scott drank too much. It was clear to the Murphys and anyone else who spent time with them that summer that both Fitzgeralds were emotionally and physically exhausted, sick of each other and their life together.

Fragile and thin, Zelda stretched her body to its breaking point in her pursuit of a career as a dancer and was offered a position with the San Carlos Ballet Opera Company in Naples in September of 1929. This offer included solo roles and would have given Zelda the status of a professional ballet dancer. It was a very good offer for a woman of Zelda's age and lack of professional experience but, inexplicably, she turned it down.

By April 1930 Zelda had reached a breaking point in her life. After trying to grab the steering wheel from Scott as he was driving them from the Riviera to Paris and attempting to swerve the car off a cliff, Zelda returned to her ballet classes with Madam Egorova. Soon, even Zelda's ballet teacher became worried about her hysteria, her hallucinations and frightening behavior. Scott knew he must take action and in May 1930 he booked Zelda into a psychiatric hospital named Les Rives des Prangins on Lake Geneva. At first Zelda insisted that she was quite well and had to return to Paris immediately to continue her ballet studies but doctors' reports suggest that Zelda was largely incoherent and visits from Scott only encouraged her to become agitated. Later it became clear from Zelda's own writing that she felt that she had lost everything. As it became clear that Zelda would never be a great ballerina and that the chance to excel as an individual had passed her by she saw no reason to go on. Zelda was diagnosed as schizophrenic and committed to a long stay in at Les Rives de Prangins.

Chapter 8

Les Rives de Prangins

The Prangins hospital was set in luxurious grounds and in many ways resembled a holiday resort. The hospital was ran by Dr Oscar Forel who lived with his family in one of the villas on the grounds. During the first weeks of her stay at Prangins, Zelda constantly tried to get her doctors and Scott to agree to releasing her. One day, Zelda even tried to run away when walking the grounds with her nurse. Zelda also urged Scott to write to Madam Egorova for a frank summation of her skills as a dancer. The reply Scott received was just as everyone had thought; Zelda had natural talent but could never compete with her best students who had been studying since they were children. Whether Scott shared this information with Zelda or not is hard to discern but it seems that being forced to let go of her dreams of being a leading ballerina fueled Zelda's madness.

Gradually Zelda was able to admit that she needed psychiatric help but struggled to untangle her own destructive behavior from Scott's. Many of Zelda's letters to Scott at this time are accusing, bringing up his excessive drinking as a catalyst for her escape from their life together. She also expresses her desire to find purpose in her life, saying, 'I want to work at something, but I can't seem to get well enough to be of any use in the world.' In return, Scott's letters are at times conciliatory, at times accusing. Scott also exchanged letters with Dr Forel, in which he analyzed his marriage to Zelda. Although Scott desired to get to the root of Zelda's psychiatric problems, he was unwilling to admit that he may have had a hand in her decline.

Significantly, Scott also refused to acknowledge that he had a drinking problem. As Scott explains it, he began drinking during the day due to pressure from Zelda to 'be gay'. Scott made reference to his low blood pressure and indicated that a moderate amount of wine, 'a pint with each meal', made all the difference in how he felt and his ability to write. To give up alcohol completely would be, he felt, illogical and unnecessary, even if it would help Zelda to recover. Scott suggested that in asking him to stop drinking Zelda was shifting blame for her illness and trying to prove that his alcoholism caused it. He also harshly criticized Zelda for her obsession with dancing and insisted that 'people respected her (Zelda) because I concealed her weaknesses.'

The stress of Zelda's breakdown caused her skin to erupt in painful eczema, a condition she had experienced before but never as severely as she did during her time at Prangins. Zelda's eczema felt like torture and she was subject to a number of experimental cures to rid it, including being bound in bandages and kept in bed for over a month at a time. Zelda begged Scott to help her, to explain the roots of her illness, cure her and release her from her confinement in the sanatorium. Strangely, the only thing that in any way alleviated Zelda's eczema was hypnosis, performed by Dr Forel. Scott moved to Lausanne and began visiting Zelda one a week but visits from Scottie, who was living with a nanny in Paris, were deemed too upsetting.

Eventually Scottie did visit, around Christmas 1930 but Zelda's condition had deteriorated and she behaved erratically, smashing ornaments from the Christmas tree and babbling. Soon after Christmas Scott's father died in Washington. The death was sudden and Scott was grief-stricken. Before leaving for America to attend his father's funeral, Scott visited Zelda who was herself upset at the loss. Scott suggested to Dr Forel before he left that Zelda might benefit from some form of physical exercise. Handcrafts were a challenge for Zelda as she had poor eyesight and found any repetitive activity dull so Zelda took up skiing. Her condition improved dramatically as she began to eat with the other patients, stopped having episodes of violent behavior and incoherence and began to look visibly more happy and serene. Physical activity had certainly improved Zelda's condition but it's possible that Scott's absence also had a positive effect.

in spring and through into summer Zelda made a steady, gradual recovery. As her condition improved she was allowed greater privileges, such as spending weekends with Scott and taking trips to Geneva and Lausanne with other patients. In July Zelda was able to spend two enchanted weeks with Scott and Scottie in Annecy and in August the three holidayed with the Murphys in the Austrian Tyrol. Both trips passed by beautifully with Zelda grateful to be back in the world. By September it was time for Zelda to be discharged from Prangins and integrated fully back into society. She had been institutionalized for one year and three months.

The summary of Zelda's condition on her discharge makes for interesting reading. Dr Forel wrote that Zelda's psychiatric problems were the result of feelings of inferiority, primarily in relation to Scott and that she had ambitions for herself that were self-deceptions and had caused a rift in her marriage. Overall, if Zelda behaved and did not have any more self-deceptions, she would make a full recovery.

Chapter 9

Breakdown and Recovery

The Fitzgeralds travelled to Paris then boarded a liner bound for America. From New York the Fitzgeralds travelled to Montgomery so that Zelda could be close to her family and decided to buy a house there. Predictably, both Zelda and Scott soon felt uncomfortable in the small Alabama town where, as Zelda said, nothing had happened since the Civil War. Zelda felt alienated from the other women in Montgomery, whose life experience was so much smaller than hers. For Scott's part, he found life in Montgomery interminably dull and the pressure of monitoring Zelda's behavior for tell-tale signs of her illness returning while working on his novel began overwhelm him.

Soon Scott had an excuse to leave Montgomery in the form of a job opportunity in Hollywood. After his failure in 1927 Scott was keen to make a name for himself as a screenwriter and the money was too good to turn down. While Scott was away Zelda focused on her writing. In just eight weeks Zelda managed to write seven short stories and begin work on a novel, although she encountered difficulties selling her work. Sadly only one of the stories, *Miss Ella*, was published in Scribners in December 1931 and nothing survives of the other six. Zelda's fiction was heavily descriptive and focused on love, success and beauty, as it had done before her breakdown. But her difficulty in creating memorable and unique characters who were moved and changed by the events that befell them stopped her work from being a huge success.

While Zelda was productive in Scott's absence she was still incredibly dependent on him and wrote him scores of letters saying how much she missed him and needed his company. She also expressed little faith in her ability as a writer, referring to most of what she wrote as junk. Zelda began to compare her work closely to Scott's own and, finding herself lacking, started back down the destructive road of feeling inferior to Scott.

On November 17th 1931 Judge Sayre died and was paid the highest honors by the State of Alabama for his work for the Department of

Justice. Zelda coped with her father's death remarkably well, considering Scott was not by her side but as the weeks of Scott's absence dragged on some of Zelda's early symptoms came back. Zelda took a solo trip to Florida where she hoped the climate would cure her asthma and eczema but she still pined terribly for Scott and her letters at this time reveal a diminished sense of self that is utterly different to the Zelda Scott had known before her illness. Even after the publication of *Miss Ella*, which created a lot of attention for Zelda in Montgomery, she wrote to Scott begging him to teach her to write and insisting that she couldn't re-read the story for fear that it was too poorly written.

Scott returned to Montgomery on the 20th of December, Christmas came and went and Zelda decided the family should move to Florida for a while. Scott agreed and the family relocated to Florida where they both intended to work on their novels. Devastatingly Zelda's eczema came back and when she began to behave strangely the pair were forced to return to Montgomery. After two bouts of hysteria, too similar to the time preceding Zelda's stay in Prangins to ignore, Scott had Zelda checked into a psychiatric clinic in Baltimore.

In Baltimore Zelda seemed to recuperate well. To curb her obsessive tendencies Zelda was permitted to write but only for two hours a day. After a few months Zelda had completed her novel and, without asking for Scott's opinion, sent it direction to Scribners for publication. When Scott learned of this his reaction was extreme. Scott was furious at what he saw as Zelda's purposeful use of his own material in her novel. Zelda had read portions of the novel that would later become *Tender is the Night* and it's true that Zelda's work was partly autobiographical but Scott failed to see that she too had a right to use her own experiences as creative expression. Scott had become so used to using Zelda's life in his work that he saw her own writing as plagiarism.

That Zelda had managed to complete her novel in just three months while Scott had worked intermittently on his for seven also rankled. Scott had to revert back to short story writing in order to raise the funds to keep their home in Montgomery and keep Zelda in the clinic and he resented her lack of responsibility. While Zelda continued her treatment in Baltimore Scott continued to fume over her novel, insisting that she make huge changes to it and remove any incidence from their lives that also appear in his work. Scott wrote to Zelda's doctor that he could not stand by and watch her build a writing career on 'morsels of living matter chipped out of my mind, my belly, my nervous system and my loins'.

Zelda signed a contract with Scribners on the 14th of June 1932 for the publication of *Save Me the Waltz*. Scott insisted that any praise of the book be send directly to him for fear of inspiring egomania in Zelda and he also organized the details of the contract, which stipulated that 50% of any earnings be kept by the publishers to pay off debt Scott owed.

There are many parallels between the lives of the characters in *Save me the Waltz* and lives of Scott and Zelda. The novel's protagonist, Alabama Beggs, is a young debutante in Alabama who marries David Knight, an artist stationed in her town during World War One. Alabama and David travel to New York and then to Paris where Alabama falls in love with a young aviator. Soon after David has an affair with a Hollywood actress. Alabama deals with the increasing feeling that she has wasted her life by training to become a ballet dancer. Alabama receives an offer to dance in Naples, which she accepts, leaving her husband and child to cope without her until an infection in her foot ruins her dancing career and she and her husband are reunited.

Zelda stayed at the clinic in Baltimore until June 1932 at which point she moved into a home Scott had rented close to the clinic. *Save me the Waltz* was published in October 1932 and did not sell well. Critical reaction was fairly negative with most reviewers noting that the writing was overly-stylized and that there was a lack of careful editing. On a positive note some reviewers praised Zelda's warmth and intelligence and signaled that the writing in *Save me the Waltz* was merely undisciplined and would improve with time. Zelda was crushed by the poor reaction to her book but coped with it well, or seemed to.

Zelda tried to build on *Save me the Waltz* in the fall of 1932 when she began work on a new novel that would deal with her experience of schizophrenia. Scott was furious that Zelda was continuing to write using material from her own life. The tension in the Fitzgerald home became palpable as Zelda struggled to maintain her fragile mental health and Scott, still struggling to finish *Tender is the Night*, drank more than ever.

The Fitzgeralds attended weekly sessions at Phipps where they talked over their problems with psychiatrists. In one session that was transcribed by a stenographer, Scott unleashed his fury at Zelda.

Scott blamed Zelda entirely for the eight year gap in his career as a novelist pointing to years she was sick and the years she studied ballet as stopping him from working. He coldly pointed out the difference between a professional writer and an amateur and added, 'you are a third-rate writer and a third-rate ballet dancer'. Scott made it clear that as the professional writer of the two, everything in he and Zelda's life together and indeed Zelda's life before they even met, was his material. Scott told Zelda in no uncertain terms to stop writing fiction and Zelda reacted by stating that she wanted to be independent of Scott in every way. In her typically elliptical way, Zelda said, 'I want to be, to say, when he says something that is not so, then I want to do something so good, that I can say, 'that is a bad damned lie!' and have something to back it up, that I can say it.'

In the middle of July Zelda's brother Anthony committed suicide and life in the Fitzgerald household became more intolerable by the day.

Scott was locked away in his office making *Tender is the Night* ready for publication in January 1934 and Zelda spent the majority of her time painting. Some of these paintings were exhibited at the gallery of the Fitzgerald's friend, Cary Ross in New York.

The exhibition, although well received seemed to contribute to a relapse and Zelda moved back into Phipps full time in February 1934. Zelda's condition steadily grew worse. She refused to get out of bed, refused to eat, entered catatonic states and her writing became, at times, illegible. Zelda was moved to an expensive hospital in New York then back to a different hospital in Baltimore, growing more confused and dispirited all the time. As 1935 rolled into view the Fitzgeralds lost hope that Zelda could ever get better. A plan to pull together a collection of her short fiction, including the short stories she had published in College Humor and her published articles came to nothing. Eventually Zelda told Scott and her doctors that she wanted to take her own life.

Chapter 10

The Last Romantics

Scott was still vaguely functioning as an alcoholic and in 1936 moved Zelda to the Highland Hospital in Asheville, North Carolina. As Zelda approached her 36th birthday her condition seemed to improve and Scott remarked that she looked five years younger and healthier than she had for years. Although, Zelda still struggled to separate reality from fantasy and was only permitted to leave the hospital to meet Scott for lunch nearby, an arrangement they carried out once every few months. By now Scott was in dire straits financially and his health began to fail.

In a last ditch attempt to get himself on solid financial footing, Scott took a job in Hollywood writing for MGM on a salary of $1000 a month. Scott came into contact with people he hadn't seen for years and many were shocked by the physical change in him. However, Scott's charm was still effective enough to attract women and during his first week in Hollywood he began an affair with a journalist named Sheilah Graham. Those who had known Zelda in her youth noted the similarity between Zelda and Sheila's appearance. Sheilah was like a breath of fresh air for Scott and in the first flushes of new romance his grief over Zelda's insanity wavered. Scott lost pity for Zelda and a family reunion with Zelda and Scottie in March 1938 to Virginia Beach was a disaster. To deal with the strain Scott again became violently drunk and was hospitalized on his return to Hollywood.

When Scott made it clear that he would no longer shoulder sole responsibility for Zelda's welfare she became desperate to leave the hospital and return to her family in Montgomery. It was clear to Zelda's doctors that she could not take care of herself and Mrs Sayre's' insistence that Zelda be released into her care infuriated Scott. In February 1939, Scott caused a repeat of the disastrous holiday of March 1938 when he took Zelda to Cuba on a drunken whim fueled by a violent quarrel with his mistress, Shielah. This time Scott was hospitalized for two weeks on his return because of his drinking. Now, all but beaten by his alcoholism and almost penniless, Scott began work on *The Last Tycoon.*

Finally, in March 1940, four years after entering the Highland Hospital, Zelda was released and allowed to go home to Montgomery. Zelda was now forty years old and as she boarded the bus to Montgomery she was buoyed by the sense of a new beginning but it soon became clear that her life in Montgomery was not going to be the fresh start she had hoped for. Exhausted by the pressure of conforming to a schedule that would stop the symptoms of her schizophrenia returning, Zelda had no energy for anything else. Friends she had known were estranged and keeping up with her promise to her doctors to walk 5 miles every day she was considered a town oddity.

Zelda's isolated life resembled that of a much older woman and Scott tried in vain to encourage her to paint and write. Scott's life in the west with Sheilah Graham was also quiet and he was deeply committed to completing *The Last Tycoon*. In November 1940, after suffering a number of minor 'cardiac spasms' F. Scott Fitzgerald had a heart attack and died in Shielah Graham's apartment. Zelda had not seen Scott for a year and a half and at first did not believe that he was dead. Zelda did not go to Scott's funeral and once grief fully set in Zelda became more isolated than ever. Scott had always acted as a conduit between Zelda and the rest of the world and with him gone it seemed there was no one alive who understood her. For Zelda, only the remembrance of her and Scott's magnificent youth was worth living for.

The Last Tycoon was published posthumously and included in a volume of Scott's work published in October 1941. In 1942 Zelda began to write again and began a novel she named *Caesar's Things.* Although unfinished this novel is largely autobiographical but differs from *Save me the Waltz* in its theme of religious fervor. Unfortunately Zelda's strong ideas on religion and living a 'biblical life' were a clear symptom of her illness and what she wrote in *Caesar's Things* is largely fantastical, full of religious fervor without context and incoherent. Zelda also continued to draw and paint after Scott's death and her work was exhibited by the Museum of Fine Arts in May 1942.

Scottie was married in February 1943 to Lieutenant Samuel Jackson Lanahan who was sent overseas immediately after the ceremony. Zelda did not attend the wedding but was invited to spend two weeks in New York with Scottie in the summer of 1943. This trip was to be the high point of Zelda's final years as she spent 1944 to

1946 in and out of Asheville, overcome by religious zeal. Zelda believed herself to be communing directly with God and wrote short essays to her friends in an attempt to save their souls. In April 1946 Zelda became a grandmother when Scottie gave birth to a baby boy, Timothy Lanahan. Zelda was thrilled but noted that she found it incredible that anyone of her generation should be a grandmother.

On November 2nd 1947 Zelda made the trip back to the Highland hospital for the very last time. On March 10th 1948 a fire broke out in the hospital kitchen. Each of the floors of the hospital was equipped with a dumbwaiter and the fire spread up the shafts with ease. Zelda was sleeping on the main floor of the hospital when the fire broke out. She was unable to escape and fire crews were hampered in their rescue efforts by locked doors and barred windows. Nine women including Zelda died in the fire. Zelda was buried on the 17th of March 1948 in Maryland, alongside Scott.

Conclusion

At the time of her death Zelda was penniless and living between her mother's home and a mental institution. Scott had been dead for eight years, Zelda was unable to live without supervision and there was no hope of her ever making a full recovery.

In most retellings of Zelda's life the long period of her illness is skipped over or quickly summarized. It's certainly more palatable to focus on the best years of Zelda's life but in reality a large part of Zelda's life was spent in psychiatric care. Zelda was first hospitalized in April 1930 and her illness dominated 18 years of her life and 10 years of her 20-year marriage to Scott. Directly following her death Zelda's life was considered desperately tragic. Zelda's celebrity was short-lived and dependent on her marriage to Scott and once the Fitzgeralds had slid out of the public eye and the great Jazz Age was over no one thought too much about Zelda much anymore.

People forgot Zelda's wild and misspent youth in Montgomery, where she was the epitome of the Southern belle in looks and social standing but too much of a free spirit to really fit in. They forgot the early years of her marriage to Scott, during which time she became the most sought-after party guest in New York City. They forgot the time she spent flying from place to place, living in rented villas on the French Riviera, luxurious apartments in Paris or mansions in various cities in America. Above all people forgot the time when everyone wanted to be close to the Fitzgeralds, to feel some of that sense of freedom, extravagance and wit, that looked remarkably like gold-dust rub off from the Fitzgerald's sun kissed faces and on to them.

Then, in 1970 Nancy Milford wrote a Pulitzer Prize nominated biography of Zelda's life and interest in her story, with Scott as merely one facet of it, was awakened. Gradually people realized that Zelda's life was as significant to American literary history as Scott's, perhaps even more so given the extent to which her life inspired his fiction. Zelda feared that her life had no meaning, that she was not accomplished enough, that her work was not good enough. Zelda feared that her lifelong commitment to live on her own terms, free of hypocrisy, free of repression, free of the mundane, had been made in vain. As she lived on a tight regime, constantly watched by psychiatrists, it must have certainly felt that way. But Zelda's influence stretched further than the limits of her own time here and her unique legacy lives on, growing stronger with the passing of time.

In 1975, Scott and Zelda's daughter had their bodies moved to Scott's family plot at the Saint Mary's Catholic Cemetery. Their tombstone is inscribed with words that will be familiar to any F. Scott Fitzgerald fan, 'so we beat on, boats against the current, borne back, ceaselessly into the past.'

Made in the USA
Middletown, DE
13 November 2018